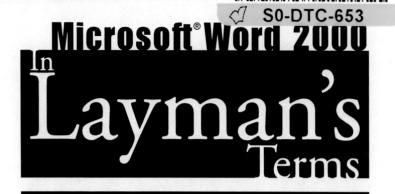

Microsoft® Word 2000
In Layman's Terms

By Katie Layman

Computers Made Easy, Hollister, California

> *In loving memory of my Dad, John J. Layman,*
> *whose zest for life continues to inspire me.*

Microsoft® Word 2000 In Layman's Terms
by Katie Layman

Design and Desktop Publishing: Paul A. Wiren

Cover Graphics: Ruben Cota

Copyediting: Deborah Leighton, Maine Proofreading Services

Keystroke Testing: Deborah Miles

Executive Assistant: Elizabeth Guerrero

Published by:
Computers Made Easy
Post Office Box 98
Hollister, CA 95024-0098 U.S.A.

Printed in the United States of America

Library of Congress Card Number: 00-100245

Contents

Preface, vii

Editing Text
Select (Highlight) a Word, 1
Select (Highlight) a Paragraph, 1
Select (Highlight) All Text, 1
Select (Highlight) a Sentence, 1
Select (Highlight) One Line, 1
Extend a Selection, 2
Delete Text, 2
Insert Text, 3
Move to the End of a Document, 3
Move to the Beginning of a Document, 3
Copy Text Using Drag & Drop, 3
Move Text Using Drag & Drop, 3

Document Creation and Protection
Open a New Window, 4
Open an Existing Document, 4
Close All Windows, 4
Protect Documents (Save with a Password), 4
Open a Password-Protected File, 5
Remove a Password, 6
Create Multiple Versions of a Document, 6
Save a Document, 7

Use Special Features
Help Wizard Assistant, 8
Change Margins, using the Page Setup dialog box, 9
Use the Memo Wizard, 10
Replace Text, 10
Use the Undo and Redo Commands, 11

Bullet or Number a List, 11

Indent Text, 12

Print Envelope Address, 13

Create WordArt, 14

Insert and Modify a Table
Create a Table, 14

Insert a Table Row, 15

Delete a Table Row, 15

Insert a Table Column, 15

Delete a Table Column, 16

Move a Column, 16

Remove Table Borders, 17

Merge Table Cells, 17

Display a Different Toolbar, 17

Change Column Widths, 18

Set Row Height, 18

Center a Table Horizontally and Vertically, 19

Sort Table Rows, 19

Calculate a Column or Row Total, 20

Use Single or Double Underlines, 21

Manage Words and Pages
Create Newspaper-Style Columns, 21

Use Format Painter, 22

Use Shrink to Fit, 22

Use Word Count, 22

Check Spelling, 23

Use the Grammar Feature, 24

Use the Thesaurus, 24

Change Vertical Line Spacing, 25

Number Pages Automatically, 25

Manage Files

Use the Open or Save Dialog Box to Copy, Move (Cut), and Rename Files, 26

Use Send To, 27

Create a New Folder, 27

Delete a File, 27

Find Files, 27

Use the Favorites Folder, 28

Create Multi-page Documents and Use Merging

Create a Header with a Page Number, 28

Create a Footer with a Date and the Page Number, 29

Create a Data source File (Database) for a Form Letter, 30

Create a Main Document (Form Letter), 32

Merge the Main Document with a Data Source File, 33

Create Labels from a Data Source (Database) File, 34

Create a Cross-reference in a Master Document for a Bookmark, 35

Use Special Functions

Use AutoCorrect, 36

Use AutoFormat, 37

Create a Letterhead with Borders, 37

Create a Flier Using AutoShapes, 38

Use AutoText, 39

Create a Superscript or Subscript, 40

Create, Run, and Delete Macros, 40

Track Changes in a Document, 42

Insert and View Comments, 43

Create a Read-Only Document, 44

Use Additional Features

Customize Toolbars, 44

Change Margins, Using the Ruler, 45

Use Click & Type, 46

Change Font Size and/or Appearance, 46

Insert a Picture (Graphic Image), 46

Create a New Template Based on an Existing Template, 47

Set Tabs Using the Horizontal Ruler, 48

Set Tabs using the Tabs Dialog Box, 49

Control Text Flow, 50

Create Bookmarks, 51

Go to a Bookmark, 51

Create a Watermark, 52

Use Hidden Text, 54

Collect and Paste Items to the Clipboard, 55

Glossary, g1

Index, i1

Toolbars, t1

Order Forms

Preface

The Microsoft® Word 2000 In Layman's Terms reference guide was created as a result of many requests from my clients and students to have a quick step-by-step instruction guide for using the major features of one of the world's most popular word processing programs, Microsoft Word. This easy-to-follow guide is a hands-on approach designed for the novice as well as the experienced Microsoft Word user.

Included in this quick reference guide are step-by-step instructions for many of the Microsoft Word functions. Also included are many figures that illustrate the option or dialog box specified in the procedure(s).

What's in this reference guide?
Step-by-step instructions for:

➤ Creating and modifying tables

➤ Calculating a column or row total

➤ Creating newspaper-style columns

➤ Using bullets and numbers

➤ Creating multiple versions of a document

➤ Merging letters

➤ Printing envelope addresses and labels

➤ Modifying and enhancing documents

➤ Inserting graphics

➤ Using AutoText, AutoCorrect, and AutoFormat

➤ Creating a letterhead with borders

➤ Setting tabs

➤ Using Wizards

➤ And much more...

What are the major features of this reference guide?

➤ Thorough step-by-step hands-on instructions

➤ Figures to visually illustrate the instructions provided

➤ Efficient steps for performing popular tasks

➤ Shortcut instructions when available

Who should use *In Layman's Terms?*

➤ Beginning as well as advanced users of the Microsoft® Word 2000 program

➤ Users who want to update their skills to the Word 2000 program

➤ Users who need a refresher on how to perform Word functions

How can *In Layman's Terms* be used?

➤ To perform computer tasks on the job with Microsoft Word 2000

➤ In a training seminar

➤ In business offices

➤ As a refresher on using Word features

➤ To review the standard Word functions

➤ As a supplement to any comprehensive Word 2000 reference book

Acknowledgments

Paul W. Wiren, once again thank you for developing and desktop-publishing my books. Many thanks to Wanda Wong and Victor Cheng at Photo Type Typesetting for taking over the process of desktop-publishing the final copies of my books.

Debbie Leighton at Maine Proofreading Services, you are commended for your accurate and thorough copyediting of this manuscript. I appreciate your positive attitude and loyalty to this project.

An enormous thank you is extended to Deborah Miles who provided many comments and suggestions for improving the step-by-step instructions. Your thoroughness and dedication to this project are very much appreciated.

I send a heartfelt thanks to Elizabeth Guerrero, my Executive Assistant, who has been the expert in handling all phases of producing this reference guide. You assisted with creating, editing, proofreading, organizing, and keeping this project moving! I can't thank you enough!

A special thank-you is extended to my reviewers. Susan Ashcraft, Trainer, Scientific Games, Inc., thanks for providing ideas for a marketable pricing structure. Ron Martin, PostNet, thank you for reminding me of features to include with the reference guide. Donald Shenk, Executive Assistant, Dreamworks, Inc., your thorough review provided improvement to the manuscript in content, explanations, and completeness. Lydia Keuser, San Jose City College, thank you for being willing to take time to review the manuscript in spite of a very busy schedule. Your comments from a teachers point of view were greatly appreciated.

Warning-Disclaimer

This book is designed to provide information in regard to the subject matter covered.

Every effort has been made to make this reference guide as complete and as accurate as possible. However, there may be unintentional mistakes both typographical and in content. Therefore, this text should be used as a general guide and not as the ultimate source of instructions for performing the steps to accomplish Microsoft Word 2000 features.

The purpose of this reference guide is to provide instructions for performing the steps to accomplish the many features available in the Microsoft Word 2000 program. The author and Computers Made Easy shall have neither liability nor responsibility to any person or entity with respect to any loss or damage caused, or alleged to be caused, directly or indirectly by the instructions contained in this reference guide.

If you do not wish to be bound by the above, this book may be returned to the publisher for a full refund.

Notes:

Microsoft® Word 2000
In Layman's
Terms

Select (Highlight) a Word
➤ Double-click on the word.

Select (Highlight) a Paragraph
➤ Triple-click on the paragraph, or point in the left margin and double-click.

Select (Highlight) All Text
➤ Point in the left margin and triple-click, or press **Ctrl + a**.

Select (Highlight) a Sentence
➤ *1.* Click on the sentence to locate the insertion point anywhere in the sentence.
➤ *2.* Press and hold the **Ctrl** key and click once.

Note: If the sentence contains another period, such as in an abbreviated word, the selection will highlight only up to that period.

Select (Highlight) One Line
➤ *1.* Point in the left margin beside the line until the right arrow pointer displays.
➤ *2.* Click once.

Extend a Selection

Method 1:

➤ *1.* Click on the left side of the text to be selected.
➤ *2.* Double-click on the shaded (grayed) **EXT** button on the Status bar.
➤ *3.* Point to the right side of the text to be selected and click once.

Note: *To turn off **Extend**, perform a task such as pressing the **Delete** key, or double-clicking on the **EXT** button in the Status bar, or pressing the **Esc** key.*

Method 2:

➤ *1.* Click on the left side of the text to be selected.
➤ *2.* Press the **Shift** key, and click on the right side of the text to be selected.

Delete Text

➤ Select (i.e., highlight) the text and press the **Delete** (**Del**) key on the keyboard.

Note: *See the instructions above for highlighting (selecting) a word, sentence, line, paragraph, or all text.*

Insert Text

➤   Place the insertion point at the location where text is to be typed and type the desired text.

Note: If the Insert (Ins) key is "on", the text will be replaced. The OVR (Overtype) button will be displayed in black letters on the Status bar located at the bottom of the document window. Press the insert key to turn off overtype. The OVR letters on the overtype button will be "grayed out."

Move to the End of a Document

➤   Ctrl+End

Move to the Beginning of a Document

➤   Ctrl+Home

Copy Text Using Drag & Drop

➤ *1.* Select the desired text to be copied.
➤ *2.* Point to the highlighted text and press the **Ctrl** key. Click & hold and drag the dotted insertion point to the desired location.
➤ *3.* Release the mouse before the **Ctrl** key is released.

Move Text Using Drag & Drop

➤ *1.* Select the desired text to be moved.
➤ *2.* Point to the highlighted text; click & hold and drag the dotted insertion point to the desired location.
➤ *3.* Release the mouse.

Open a New Window

➣ Select the **New Blank Document** button ▣ on the toolbar.

Open an Existing Document

➣ Select the **Open** button ☞ on the toolbar and double-click on the desired filename.

Close All Windows

➣ *1.* Hold the **Shift** key while clicking on the **File** menu.

➣ *2.* Choose **Close All**.

Protect Documents (Save with a Password)

➣ *1.* Select **File, Save As**.
   a) Type the desired filename.
   b) Select **Tools, General Options**.
   c) Click in the **Password to open** box located in the lower left corner of the dialog box. *See Figure 1.*

➣ *2.* Type the desired password in the **Password to open** box.

Note: To ensure privacy, the typed characters are displayed as asterisks on the screen. Remember, passwords are case-sensitive and can contain as many as 15 characters including numbers, letters, symbols, and spaces.

   d) Select **OK**.

Note: The Confirm Password dialog box appears.

    e) Type the password again in the Confirm Password dialog box.

    f) Select **OK**.

    g) If necessary, select the disk drive where your disk is located. Select **Save** in the **Save As** dialog box.

Note: You will be returned to the document window.

Figure 1.
The Save options dialog box.

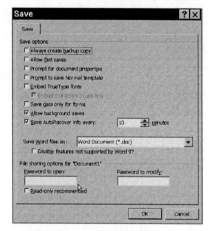

Open a Password-Protected File

➤ *1.* Select the **Open** button.

➤ *2.* Double-click on the desired filename.

Note: The Password dialog box displays.

➤ *3.* Type the password exactly as typed when the password was created.

Note: As the password is typed, asterisks display on the screen

➤ *4.* Select **OK**.

Note: The password-protected file displays.

Remove a Password

➤ *1.* With the password-required document open, select **File, Save As**.
➤ *2.* Select **Tools, General Options**.
➤ *3.* Double-click in the **Password to open** box.
➤ *4.* Press the **Delete** key.
➤ *5.* Select **OK**.
➤ *6.* Select **Save** to save the file without the password.

Create Multiple Versions of a Document

Note: Multiple versions of a document can be saved in one file. This is useful when more than one person works on the same file. Use this method to name and save the file for the first time.

➤ *1.* Select **File, Versions**.
➤ *2.* Click on **Save Now**.
➤ *3.* In the **Comments on version** box type a description for this file version.
  See Figure 2.
➤ *4.* Select **OK**.
　　a) To open the last saved version of a document, select the **Open** button and double-click on the filename desired.
　　b) To open a previously saved version of the document, select **File, Versions**.
　　c) Double-click on the desired version.

Note: Both versions of the document display in a separate document windows.

Figure 2.
Save Version dialog box.

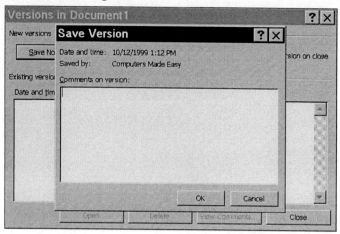

Save a Document

➤ *1.* Click on the **Save** 🖫 button located on the Standard toolbar

Note: The Save As dialog box displays.

➤ *2.* Click in the **Save in:** box and choose the location where the document is to be saved.

➤ *3.* In the **File name:** box, double-click on the suggested filename and type the desired filename. For example, type letter to Barbara Martin. (Do not type the period.)

➤ *4.* Click on the **Save** button.

*Note: To save a document with a different name, select the File menu, choose **Save As...** and follow steps 2-4 above.*

Help Wizard Assistant

*Note: The Office Assistant must be turned off. (Select **Options** in the Office Assistant box and deselect the "Use the Office Assistant" option: OK.)*

➤ 1. Select the **Help** menu.
➤ 2. Click on the **Microsoft Word Help** option.
➤ 3. Select the **Answer Wizard** tab. *See Figure 3.*
➤ 4. Type your question.
➤ 5. Click on **Search**.

Figure 3.
Microsoft Word Help dialog box.

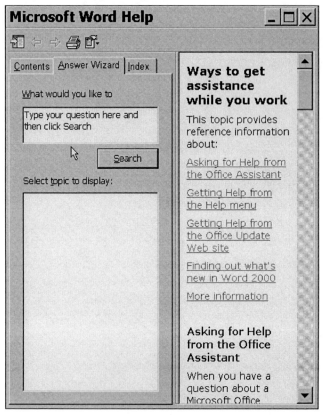

Microsoft Word 2000 In Layman's Terms

Change Margins Using the Page Setup Dialog box

➤ *1.* Select **File, Page Setup**.

➤ *2.* Choose the Margins tab. *See Figure 4.*

➤ *3.* Type the desired margins in the **Top**, **Bottom**, **Left**, and **Right** boxes (or click on the up or down arrows to increase or decrease the number displayed). Select **OK**.

Note: Also see Changing Margins Using the Ruler on page 45.

Figure 4.
Page Setup dialog box.

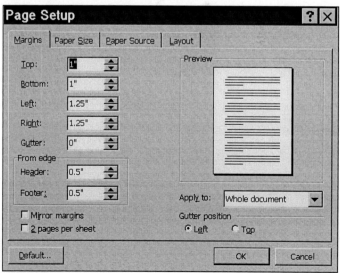

Use the Memo Wizard

➤ *1.* Select **File, New.**

➤ *2.* Choose the **Memos** tab.

➤ *3.* Select the **Memo Wizard, OK.** *See Figure 5.*

➤ *4.* Choose **Next**; select the desired style, e.g. Contemporary.

➤ *5.* Choose **Next** twice.

➤ *6.* Fill in the Date, From, and Subject boxes as needed.

➤ *7.* Select **Next.**

➤ *8.* Type the name(s) of the person(s) who are to receive the memo; choose **Next.**

➤ *9.* Type in the Writer's initials; choose **Next.**

➤*10.* Click **Next** to bypass (or accept) the header/footer information.

➤*11.* Choose **Finish.**

Figure 5.
Memo Wizard
Start window.

Replace Text

➤ *1.* Select **Edit, Replace.**

➤ *2.* Type the desired text to find in the Find what: box.

➤ *3.* Type text to replace with in the Replace with: box.

➤ *4.* Select **Replace All.**

Use the Undo and Redo Commands

➤ *1.* After the text has been deleted or inserted, select the **Undo** 🔄 button on the Standard toolbar.

Note: The last action returns to the screen, e.g., a deleted word displays again or an inserted sentence no longer displays.

➤ *2.* Select the **Undo** button again to reverse the next-to-the-last action.

➤ *3.* Select the **Redo** button 🔄 to reverse the previous undo action.

Bullet or Number a List

➤ *1.* Type the list.

➤ *2.* Select the entire list.

➤ *3.* Choose the **Bullets** 📋 or **Numbering** 📋 button on the toolbar.

To customize the bullet or number:

➤ *1.* Select **Format, Bullets & Numbering**.

➤ *2.* Choose the **Customize** button.

➤ *3.* Select the **Bullet** button in the **Customized Bulleted List** dialog box. *See Figure 6.*

➤ *4.* Click on the down arrow located in the Font box. Scroll up or down and select (**normal text**) or **Wingdings**.

➤ *5.* Select the desired symbol then **OK**.

Figure 6
Customize
Bulleted List
dialog box.

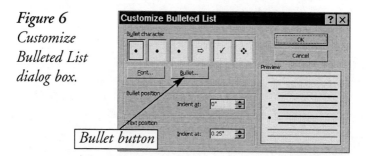

In Layman's Terms Microsoft Word 2000 11

Indent Text

➤ *1.* Select the text to be indented.

➤ *2.* Choose the **Increase Indent** button 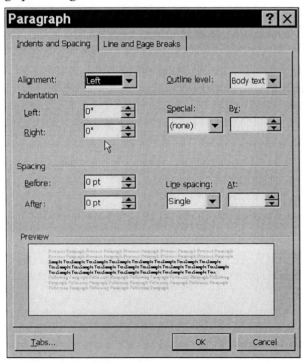 on the Formatting toolbar.

Or:

➤ *1.* Select the text.

➤ *2.* Choose **Format, Paragraph**.

➤ *3.* Select the **Indents and Spacing** tab.

➤ *4.* In the Indentation Left & Right areas, type the desired amount (or click on the up or down arrows to increase or decrease the number displayed); select *OK. See Figure 7.*

Figure 7.
Paragraph dialog box.

Microsoft Word 2000 In Layman's Terms

Print an Envelope Address

➤ *1.* With the letter containing the address displaying on the screen, choose **Tools**, **Envelopes and Labels**.

➤ *2.* In the Envelopes tab, verify that the delivery address is correct. Deselect Omit, click in the Return address box and type your return address.
See Figure 8.

➤ *3.* Select **Print** or choose **Add to Document**.

Figure 8.
Envelopes and Labels dialog box.

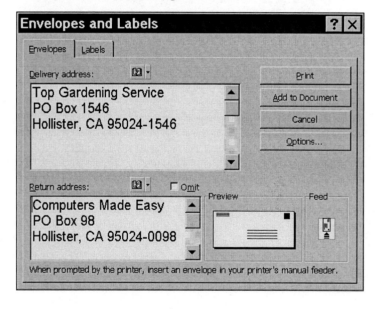

Create WordArt

➤ *1.* Select **Insert, Picture, WordArt**.
   See Figure 9.
➤ *2.* Select the desired style, click on **OK**.
➤ *3.* Type the desired text (no more than
   3 short lines recommended).

*Note: Before editing the WordArt object, the object must be selected. Double-click on the object or select the **Edit Text** button on the WordArt toolbar.*

Figure 9.
WordArt Gallery dialog box.

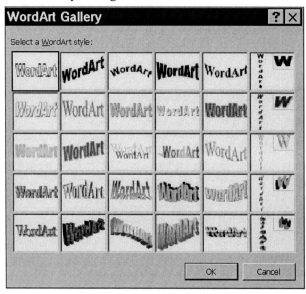

Create a Table

➤ *1.* Select the **Insert Table** button on the
   Standard toolbar.
➤ *2.* Choose the number of columns and rows
   desired.

*Note: The table borders display. If the table borders are turned off, table gridlines can be displayed by selecting **Table, Show Gridlines**.*

Microsoft Word 2000 In Layman's Terms

Insert a Table Row

➤ *1.* Highlight the row below where the row is to be inserted. (Point to the left of the row—outside the table border—until a right-pointing arrow displays; click the right mouse button once.) *See Figure 10.*

➤ *2.* Select the **Insert Rows** option.

Figure 10.
Pop-up menu
and
highlighted row.

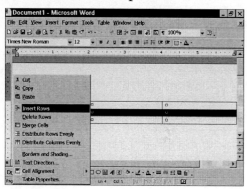

Delete a Table Row

➤ *1.* In Print Layout View, highlight the row to be deleted. (Point to the left of the row—outside the table border—until a right-pointing arrow displays; click once.)

➤ *2.* Right-mouse click on the selected row.

➤ *3.* Choose the **Delete Rows** option.

Insert a Table Column

➤ *1.* In Print Layout View, touch the mouse pointer on the border above the column and to the right of the column where the new column is to be inserted until a down arrow displays.

➤ *2.* Right-mouse click to highlight the column and to display a pop-up shortcut menu.

➤ *3.* Choose **Insert Columns**.

Delete a Table Column

➤ *1.* In Print Layout View, touch the mouse pointer on the border above the column to be deleted until a down arrow displays. *See Figure 11.*

➤ *2.* Right-mouse click to highlight the column and to display a pop-up shortcut menu.

➤ *3.* Choose **Delete Columns**.

Figure 11.
Down arrow above table column

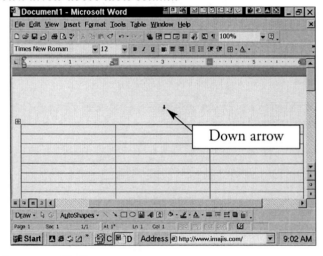

Move a Column

➤ *1.* In Print Layout View, touch the mouse pointer on the border above the column to be moved until a down arrow displays; click once to select the column.

➤ *2.* Point on the highlighted column. Click and hold the mouse button and drag the dotted insertion point to the column that will be to the right of the moved column.

➤ *3.* Release the mouse button.

Remove Table Borders

➤ 1. Select the entire table. (With the insertion point in any table cell, choose **Table, Select, Table.**)

➤ 2. Select the **Borders** button  on the Formatting toolbar.

➤ 3. Select the **No Border** option.

Merge Table Cells

➤ 1. Select the cells to be merged by moving the mouse pointer inside the left cell border until the right-pointing arrow displays. Press and hold the mouse button while dragging the mouse to select the cells.

➤ 2. Choose **Table, Merge Cells.**

Display a Different Toolbar

➤ 1. Touch any toolbar with the mouse pointer.

➤ 2. Click the right mouse button to pop up a list of toolbars. *See Figure 12.*

➤ 3. Select the desired toolbar.

Figure 12.
List of
Toolbars.

Change Column Widths

➤ *1.* Place the mouse pointer on the vertical line between columns until a double-headed arrow appears.

➤ *2.* Click, hold, and drag the line left or right to increase or decrease the column width.

Set Row Height

➤ *1.* Place the insertion point in the row to be changed.

➤ *2.* Select **Table**, **Properties**. *See Figure 13.*

➤ *3.* Choose the **Row** tab. Click on the Specify height option. Select the down arrow in the **Row height is:** box, and choose **At least**.

➤ *4.* In the **Specify height:** box, type the desired height; select **OK**.

Figure 13.
Table
Properties
dialog box.

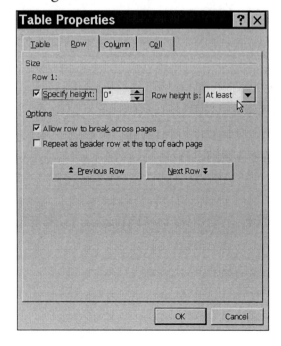

Center a Table Horizontally and Vertically

To center a table horizontally:

➤ *1.* With the insertion point in any table cell, select **Table, Properties**. Select the **Table** tab.

➤ *2.* Choose the **Center** option in the Alignment: area. Select **OK**.

To center a table vertically:

➤ *1.* With the insertion point in any table cell, select **File, Page Setup**.

➤ *2.* Choose the **Layout** tab, click in the Vertical alignment box, and choose **Center**.

➤ *3.* Select **OK**.

Note: If text is on the page with the table, both the table and text are vertically centered.

Sort Table Rows

➤ *1.* Highlight the rows in the table to be sorted (but don't highlight any rows containing titles or column headings).

➤ *2.* Select **Table, Sort**.

➤ *3.* In the Sort by box, click on the down arrow and choose the Column number desired.

➤ *4.* If necessary, select a different type, i.e., Text or Number.

➤ *5.* Check that Ascending is selected.

➤ *6.* Choose **OK**.

Calculate a Column or Row Total

➤ *1.* To calculate a column total, select the cell that will contain the formula results.

➤ *2.* Select **Table, Formula**. *See Figure 14.*

➤ *3.* In the Formula: box, type in or check that the formula =**Sum(above)** is displayed.

➤ *4.* Click on the down arrow beside the Number format: box and select the **$#,##0.00;($#,##0.00)** format. Select **OK**.

Note: *To total a row, type the formula =**Sum(left)** in the Formula: box.*

Figure 14.
Formula dialog box.

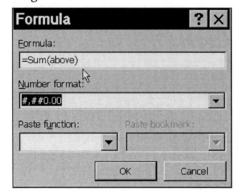

Microsoft Word 2000 In Layman's Terms

Use Single or Double Underlines

Note: If table borders are removed, a single underline is usually placed between the last column amount and the total amount. A double underline is placed beneath the total amount.

➤ 1. Highlight the cells in the row that will contain the single or double underlines.

*Note: To insert single underlines, choose the **Underline** button. To insert double underlines, select **Format, Font**. See Figure 15.*

➤ 2. Choose the **Font** tab and click in the **Underline style** box.

➤ 3. Choose the double underline style; select **OK**.

Figure 15. Font dialog box.

Double Underline style

Create Newspaper-Style Columns

➤ 1. Type all the text that will be placed in columns.

➤ 2. Highlight all the text (but don't highlight a title); select the **Columns** button on the Standard toolbar.

➤ 3. Choose the second column option.

*Note: The text displays in columns. If the columns don't display, choose the **Print Layout View** button on the vertical scroll bar.*

Use Format Painter

Note: This feature is used to copy the format from one text item to another. Therefore, a document should contain side headings and a few paragraphs.

➤ *1.* Select the formatted text from which the format is to be copied.
➤ *2.* Double-click on the **Format Painter** button 🖌.
➤ *3.* Select the text where the formatting is to be copied.
➤ *4.* Repeat for additional text.

*Note: Select the **Format Painter** button once to turn off Format Painter.*

Use Shrink to Fit

Note: Use this feature to fit a multi-page document on one less page.

➤ *1.* Select the **Print Preview** button.
➤ *2.* Select the **Shrink to Fit** button 🗏.
➤ *3.* Select the **Close Preview** button.

Use Word Count

Note: This feature is used to count the number of words, characters, or pages in a document or selected text.

➤ *1.* With the insertion point displaying at any location in a document, select **Tools**, **Word Count**.

Note: The Word Count dialog box displays.

➤ *2.* Select **Close** to return to the document window.

Check Spelling

➤ *1.* Move the mouse pointer to the first word marked with a red wavy line.

➤ *2.* Click the right mouse button to display a list of suggested words. *See Figure 16.*

➤ *3.* Select the correctly spelled word.

➤ *4.* Continue to review the document for words marked with a red wavy line.

➤ *5.* If the correct spelling of a word is not on the list, the word can be corrected by double-clicking on the word and typing the word correctly.

Figure 16.
Spelling pop-up list with suggested words.

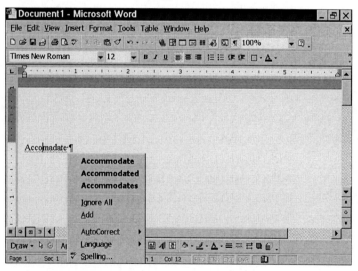

Use the Grammar Feature

Note: The document to be grammar-checked must be saved and displayed in the document window.

➤ *1.* Select **Tools**, **Options**, **Spelling & Grammar** tab.

➤ *2.* Select or deselect the Grammar options as desired.

➤ *3.* Right-mouse click on any word(s) that has a green wavy line beneath it.

➤ *4.* Select the correct word(s), or choose the **Ignore** or **Grammar** option.

➤ *5.* If the Grammar option is selected, the Grammar dialog displays. If desired, move the Grammar dialog box display. (Move the mouse pointer to the dialog box title bar. Press and hold the mouse button and drag the box down and to the right.)

➤ *6.* Select **Ignore** if the sentence is correct.

Use the Thesaurus

➤ *1.* Locate the insertion point in the word that will be looked up in the Thesaurus.

➤ *2.* Select **Tools**, **Language**, **Thesaurus**.

➤ *3.* Look at the words listed under the heading Meanings: and choose a word closest to the meaning of the word in the sentence.

➤ *4.* Select **Replace,** or select **Cancel** if no word is an appropriate choice.

Change Vertical Line Spacing

> ➤ 1. Select all lines in the text to be changed.
> ➤ 2. Choose **Format**, **Paragraph**.
> ➤ 3. Click in the Line spacing: box and select 1.5 lines or select any other option desired; choose **OK**.

*Shortcut: With the text highlighted, press **Ctrl+2** for double spacing, **Ctrl+1** for single spacing, or **Ctrl+5** for 1.5 line spacing.*

Number Pages Automatically

> ➤ 1. Select **Insert**, **Page Numbers**.
> ➤ 2. Choose the position and alignment desired. Look at the Preview on the right.
> ➤ 3. Select **OK**.

Use the Open or Save Dialog Box to Copy, Move (Cut), and Rename Files

➤ *1.* In the Open or Save dialog box, right-mouse click on the filename desired. *See Figure 17.*

➤ *2.* Choose the **Copy**, **Cut**, or **Rename** option.

To copy or cut a file:

➤ Select the folder or drive from the Look in or Save in box that will contain the copied or cut document. Right-mouse click on a folder name (or if a drive is chosen, right-mouse click in an empty area of the Open or Save dialog box). Choose **Paste** to copy or move the file to the selected folder or drive.

To rename a file:

➤ Right-mouse click on the filename; type the new name and press **Enter**.

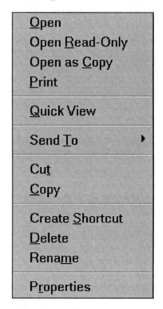

Figure 17. Shortcut menu in the Open dialog box.

Open
Open Read-Only
Open as Copy
Print

Quick View

Send To ▶

Cut
Copy

Create Shortcut
Delete
Rename

Properties

Use Send To

➤ *1.* In the Open or Save dialog box, right-mouse click on the filename desired.

➤ *2.* Select **Send To.**

➤ *3.* Select the destination desired, e.g., **3 ½ Floppy A:.**

Create a New Folder

➤ *1.* In the Save As dialog box, select the **Create a New Folder** button 🗀.

➤ *2.* Type the new folder name.

➤ *3.* Press **Enter,** or select **OK.**

Delete a File

➤ In the Open or Save dialog box, right-mouse click on the filename and choose **Delete.** Select **Yes.**

Find Files

➤ *1.* Right-mouse click on the **Start** button. Select **Find.**

➤ *2* Type the desired filename, or click in the Containing text: drop-down box and type a word(s) contained in the file.

➤ *3.* Click on the down arrow in the Look in: box and select where you want the computer to search.

➤ *4.* Choose **Find Now.**

Note: If any files are found, they are listed at the bottom of the Find dialog box, The number of documents found is shown at the bottom left of the Find dialog box.

➤ *5.* Double-click on the file to be opened.

Use the Favorites Folder

In the Save dialog box:

➤ Click on the **Favorites** button ▣, type a filename (if necessary), select **Save**.

In the Open dialog box:

➤ Click on the **Favorites** button ▣; double-click on the desired filename to open the document.

Note: *A document from a different folder can be copied or moved to Favorites. Right-mouse click on the filename, select **cut** or **copy**, click on the **Favorites** button, right-mouse click in an empty area of the Open dialog box, and choose **Paste**.*

Create a Header with a Page Number

➤ 1. Select **View, Header and Footer**.

➤ 2. Click on the **Page Setup** button on the Header and Footer toolbar. *See Figure 18 on page 29.*

➤ 3. Choose Different first page on the Layout tab.

➤ 4. Select **OK**; leave the Header area blank to *not* print a header on page 1.

➤ 5. Select the **Show Next** button ▣ on the Header and Footer toolbar.

➤ 6. Press the **Tab** key twice to locate the insertion point at the right.

➤ 7. Select the **Insert Page Number** button ▣.

Note: *Any desired text can be typed and aligned left, middle, or right in the header area.*

➤ 8. Select **Close** on the Header and Footer toolbar.

Create a Footer with a Date and the Page Number

➤ *1.* With the insertion point located on page 1, select **View, Header and Footer.**

➤ *2.* Select the **Switch Between Header and Footer** button.

➤ *3.* Select the **Insert Date** button on the Header and Footer toolbar.

➤ *4.* Press the **Tab** key twice.

➤ *5.* Select the **Insert Page Number** button.

➤ *6.* Select the **Close** button on the Header and Footer toolbar.

Note: *The information will be automatically placed in the footer on the following pages.*

Figure 18.
Header and Footer Toolbar.

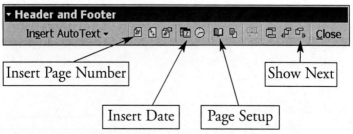

Create a Data Source File (Database) for a Form Letter

➤ *1.* Select **Tools, Mail Merge.**
➤ *2.* Choose **Create**; select **Form Letters.** *See Figure 19 on page 31.*
➤ *3.* Select the **New Main Document** button.
➤ *4.* Choose **Get Data, Create Data Source.**
➤ *5.* Click on the field names that will not be used and select the **Remove Field Name** button. For example, select **Job Title** and select the **Remove Field Name** button.
➤ *6.* Select **OK.**
➤ *7.* In the Save As box, select the folder desired and type a filename. Select **Save.**
➤ *8.* Click on **Edit Data Source.** Type the information into the Data Form box. Press the **Tab** key to move from one line (field) to the next.
➤ *9.* Select **Add New** to obtain a new Data Form.
➤ *10.* When all data are entered, select the **View Source** button. Turn on gridlines (select **Table, Show Gridlines.**)

Note: Select the Save button after any changes are made. Continue with the Create a Main Document (form letter) instructions on page 32.

Figure 19.
Mail Merge Helper dialog box.

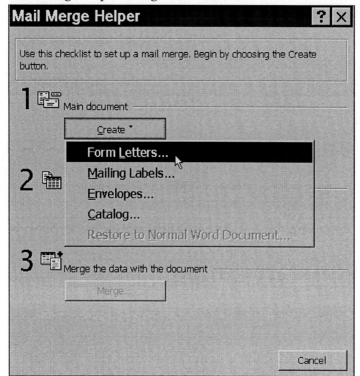

Create a Main Document (Form Letter)

➤ *1.* With the data source displayed, select the **Mail Merge Main Document** button `Merge...` located on the Mail Merge toolbar. *See Figure 20 on page 33.*

➤ *2.* Type the current date. (Or select **Insert, Date & Time.**) Press **Enter** four times.

➤ *3.* Choose the **Insert Merge Field** button `Insert Merge Field ▾` on the Mail Merge toolbar. *See Figure 21 on page 33.*

➤ *4.* Select **Title**; press the **Spacebar** once.

➤ *5.* Repeat steps 3 and 4 and insert the remaining field names and spacing/punctuation:

> FirstName; press the **Spacebar**.
> LastName; press **Enter**.
> Company; press **Enter**.
> Address1; press **Enter**.
> City; type a comma and press the **Spacebar**.
> State; press the **Spacebar**.
> PostalCode; **Enter** twice.
> Type Dear; press the **Spacebar** once.
> Select **Title**; press the **Spacebar** once.
> Select **LastName**, type a colon, and press **Enter** twice.

➤ *6.* Continue to type the remainder of your letter.

Note: Save and name your main document. Continue with the Merge the Main Document instructions with a Data Source File on Page 33.

Merge the Main Document with a Data Source File

Note: To use this feature, the data source and main document should have been created as described in the previous instructions.

➤ 1. The main document and the Mail Merge toolbar should be displayed.

➤ 2. Select the **Merge to New Document** button 🔲 on the Mail Merge toolbar. *See Figure 21.*

➤ 3. Check that the letters have merged properly; send to **Print** if desired.

Figure 20.
Mail Merge Toolbar when data source is displayed.

Figure 21.
Mail Merge Toolbar when the main document is displayed.

Merge to New Document

Create Labels from a Data Source (Database) File

Note: The data source should be created and saved.

➤ 1. In a new document, select **Tools**, **Mail Merge**.
➤ 2. Choose **Create, Mailing Labels**.
➤ 3. Click on the **Active Window** button.
➤ 4. Select **Get Data**, **Open Data Source**.
➤ 5. Double-click on the filename desired.
➤ 6. Choose **Set Up Main Document** button.
➤ 7. Select the **Laser and ink jet** option in the Printer information area.
➤ 8. Choose the Product Number desired. Select **OK**.
➤ 9. Select the **Insert Merge Field** button and choose the field names with the spacing and punctuation required for an address:

> Title; press the **Spacebar**,
> FirstName; press the **Spacebar**,
> LastName; press **Enter**.
> Company; press **Enter**.
> Address1; press **Enter**.
> City; type a comma; press **Spacebar**,
> State; press **Spacebar**,
> PostalCode; select OK to display the Mail Merge Helper dialog box.

➤ 10. Select **Close** on the Mail Merge Helper dialog box.
➤ 11. Save the new main document by selecting the **Save** button and use a filename such as Labels Main Document.
➤ 12. Choose the **Mail Merge** button on the Mail Merge toolbar.
➤ 13. Choose **Merge**.
➤ 14. The labels display and can be printed.

Note: Print first on plain paper. Place the printed labels on top of the label form and verify that the printed labels align with the label form.

Create a Cross-reference in a Master Document for a Bookmark

*Note: With the master document displayed on the screen, click on the **Outline View** button located on the left side of the horizontal scroll bar. Show all lines. (If necessary, select the **Show First Line Only** button or the **Expand Subdocuments** button on the Outlining/Master Document toolbar.) Also, a bookmark must be located on the page that will be "pointed to" by the cross-reference.*

➤ 1. Place the insertion point at the location where the reference is to be inserted in the master document.
➤ 2. Select **Insert, Cross-reference**.
➤ 3. Click in the Reference type box, and select **Bookmark**.
➤ 4. Click in the Reference to box and select **Page number**.
➤ 5. Click on the bookmark name in the **For Which Bookmark** list.
➤ 6. Select the **Insert** button.

Note: The page number is automatically inserted in the document, and the Cross-reference dialog box remains open in the document window.

➤ 7. Select **Close** to exit the Cross-reference dialog box.

Note: The page number displays in the master document.

Use AutoCorrect

➤ *1.* To display the AutoCorrect dialog box, select **Tools, AutoCorrect.**

➤ *2.* Choose or deselect the desired options.

To add a word to be changed as you type:

➤ *3.* Select **Tools, AutoCorrect.** *See Figure 22.*

➤ *4.* Click in the Replace box on the AutoCorrect tab and type the word to be changed.

➤ *5.* Click in the With box and type the desired word(s).

➤ *6.* Select the **Add** button. Select **OK.**

To check that your new AutoCorrect text works:

➤ *7.* Type the word you want changed in a document and press the **Spacebar** once.

To delete an AutoCorrect word(s):

➤ *8.* Choose **Tools, AutoCorrect.**

➤ *9.* Scroll down the item list at the bottom of the dialog box until the AutoCorrect word displays.

➤*10.* Highlight the word(s) by clicking once on the word(s); select **Delete,** then **OK.**

Figure 22.
AutoCorrect
dialog box.

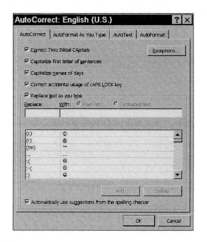

Use AutoFormat

Note: A document that uses the built-in Word styles must be created and saved.

➤ *1.* Select **Format**, **AutoFormat**. *See Figure 23.*
➤ *2.* When the AutoFormat dialog box displays, check that the AutoFormat now option is chosen; select **OK**.

Create a Letterhead with Borders

➤ *1.* Type your name. Press **Enter**.
➤ *2.* Press the **hyphen** key three times and press **Enter**. (The AutoCorrect will place a border in the document.)
➤ *3.* Type your address, phone no., fax no., and email address on separate lines.
➤ *4.* Select the lines.
➤ *5.* Select the **Align Right** button on the Formatting toolbar.

Figure 23.
AutoFormat dialog box.

Create a Flier Using AutoShapes

➤ *1.* Select **View, Print Layout.**

➤ *2.* Select the **Zoom** button and choose **Whole Page.**

➤ *3.* Select **Insert, Picture, AutoShapes.**

➤ *4.* Choose the **Basic Shapes** button 🔲 on the AutoShapes toolbar.

➤ *5.* Click on the desired shape.

➤ *6.* Move the mouse pointer (crosshair) onto the page, click at the top left of the page, and drag diagonally downward toward the bottom right of the page until the shape fills about two-thirds of the screen (exact size will be set later).

➤ *7.* Click on the **AutoShape** to select it; then right-mouse click on the shape and choose **Format AutoShape.**

➤ *8.* Select the **Size** tab. In the Size and rotate area, type 7.5 in the Height box and type **6** in the Width box.

➤ *9.* Select the **Layout** tab.

➤ *10.* Select the **Horizontal alignment and Center** options. Select **OK.**

➤ *11.* If desired, click on Line Style in the Drawing toolbar. Choose **More Lines.** Select the **Colors and Lines** tab and change the line color and fill color.

➤ *12.* Select **OK.**

To type text in the AutoShape:

➤ *13.* Click on the **AutoShape** to select it and then right-mouse click to pop up a shortcut menu.

➤ *14.* Select the **Add Text** option; type the desired text. (Choose a Zoom view of 75%.)

Note: A page border can be added by clicking on **Format, Borders and Shading** and choosing the **Page Border** tab; choose a sample border from the left side; select **OK**.

Use AutoText

Note: Use Autotext to type lines of text that are used repeatedly. For example, type the closing lines used to end your letters.

➤ 1. Type the text to be an AutoText entry.
➤ 2. Select the text and click on **Insert, AutoText, New**.
➤ 3. Type a name for the AutoText. Select **OK**.

To insert AutoText:

➤ 4. Type the AutoText name and press **F3**.

Create a Superscript or Subscript

➤ *1.* Type the desired text.

*Note: Pressing the **Tab**, **Spacebar**, or **Enter** key after the character to be a superscript or subscript makes it easier to insert additional text later.*

➤ *2.* Highlight the character to be a superscript or subscript.

➤ *3.* Select **Format, Font**. If necessary, select the **Font** tab. Select the **Superscript** or **Subscript** option in the Effects area. Select **OK**.

Note: The selected character displays as a superscript or subscript in the document window.

Create, Run, and Delete Macros

To Record a Macro:

➤ *1.* In a clear document window, select **Tools, Macro, Record New Macro**.

Note: The Record Macro dialog box displays.

➤ *2.* In the Macro name: box, type the name of the macro.

➤ *3.* Click in the Description: box at the end of the sentence that states **Macro recorded…**, and press **Enter**. Type a description of the purpose of the macro.

*Note: If desired, you can assign the macro either a toolbar or keyboard shortcut. Select the **Toolbars** 🖉 or **Keyboard** ⌨ button in the Assign macro to area.*

➤ *4.* Select **OK**.

Note: *The Stop Recording toolbar displays with Stop Recording* ⬛ *and Pause Recording* ⬛ *buttons. From now on, every keystroke or mouse selection you make will be remembered by Word until you select the Stop Recording button on the Stop Recording toolbar. A small cassette icon is attached to the mouse pointer.*

➤ 5. Perform the actions to be recorded.

➤ 6. When all actions to be recorded have been performed, select the **Stop Recording** button on the Macro Record toolbar.

Note: *The macro is automatically saved when the Stop Recording button is selected.*

To Run a Macro:

➤ 7. Press the Keyboard shortcut keys assigned to the macro, or select **Tools**, **Macro** and choose **Macros**. Double-click on the desired macro name.

Note: *The document can now be edited, saved, printed, etc., in the same manner as any other document.*

To Delete a Macro:

➤ 8. Select **Tools**, **Macro** and choose **Macros**.

➤ 9. Click on the macro name to be deleted.

➤ 10. Select **Delete**.

➤ 11. Select **Yes** to the message "Do you want to delete macro…?".

➤ 12. Select **Close** to exit the Macro dialog box.

Track Changes in a Document

Note: The track changes feature is used to mark text in a document when it is changed, i.e., inserted or deleted text. Open a document that will be changed.

➤ 1. Click on **Tools, Track Changes, Highlight Changes.**

➤ 2. Select **Track Changes while editing.** Check that **Highlight changes on screen** and **Highlight changes in printed document** are selected. *See Figure 24.*

➤ 3. Select **OK.**

➤ 4. Make the changes in the document.

➤ 5. To accept changes, select **Tools, Track Changes, Accept or Reject Changes.** Choose **Accept All.** Click the **Close** button to exit the **Accept or Reject Changes** dialog box.

➤ 6. To turn off tracking, repeat steps 1 and 2 and deselect the Track changes while editing option. Select **OK.**

Figure 24.
Highlight Changes dialog box.

Insert and View Comments

Note: A document with text should be open on the screen. To insert a comment, place the insertion point in the document where you want to make a comment.

➤ 1. Choose **Insert, Comment** and type your comment in the Comments From: window.

➤ 2. Select the **Close** button in the Comments From window. To view comments, turn on nonprinting characters by selecting the **Show/Hide** button.

➤ 3. Place the mouse pointer on the comment placeholder.

To print comments:

➤ Select **File, Print**; choose the **Print what:** option and select **Comments**; select **OK**. *See Figure 25.*

Figure 25.
Print what: options in the Print dialog box.

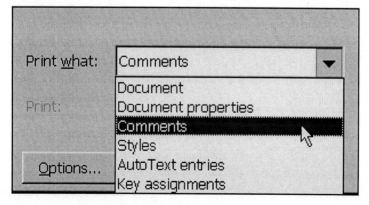

Create a Read-Only Document

➤ 1. Open the document.
➤ 2. Select **File, Save As**; choose **Tools, General Options**.
➤ 3. Select the **Read-only recommended** option box.
➤ 4. Select **OK**; select **Save**.

Note: When a read-only document is opened, select Yes to the prompt that displays "…Open as read-only?". The read-only document can be changed and saved with a different name.

Customize Toolbars

➤ 1. Point to any toolbar and right-mouse click.
➤ 2. Select the **Customize** option.
➤ 3. Choose the **Commands** tab, select the menu option in the **Categories** list. *See Figure 26.* Click on the desired button in the Commands list; then drag it out to the Toolbar.

*Note: You can also change the size of buttons displayed by choosing **Large icons** in the Options tab.*

➤ 4. Select **Close** to exit the Customize dialog box.

Figure 26.
Customize
dialog box.

Change Margins Using the Ruler

➤ *1.* Select **View, Print Layout.** (Also, verify that a checkmark displays beside the Ruler option in the View menu.)

➤ *2.* Point to the left margin on the ruler until a double-headed arrow displays and the ScreenTip displays Left Margin. *See Figure 27.*

➤ *3.* Click, hold, and drag left or right.

Note: Repeat to change the right margin using the ruler. (Also see Changing Margins Using the Page Setup dialog box on Page 9.)

Figure 27.
Left Margin ScreenTip on the Ruler.

Use Click & Type

➤ *1.* Move the mouse pointer to an empty area in the document window. For example, place the mouse pointer in the middle of the document window and double-click.

Note: The insertion point displays in the document window.

➤ *2.* Type the desired text.

Note: The text you type will begin at the new location.

Change Font Size and/or Appearance

➤ *1.* Highlight the text to be changed.
➤ *2.* Select **Format, Font.**
➤ *3.* On the Font tab, choose the desired font changes.

Note: A sample of the font and size displays in the Preview box at the bottom of the font dialog box.

➤ *4.* Select **OK.**

Insert a Picture (Graphic Image)

➤ *1.* With the insertion point at any location on the page, select **Insert, Picture, ClipArt.**
➤ *2.* On the Pictures tab, double-click on the desired category. Click on the desired picture. Select the **Insert Clip** option. Select the **Close** button on the Insert ClipArt title bar.
➤ *3.* Size and position the ClipArt as desired.

Create a New Template Based on an Existing Template

➤ *1.* Select **File**, **New**.

Note: Do not *select the New button.*

➤ *2.* In the New dialog box, select the tab that contains the icon for the template to be used as the basis for the new template. For example, click on the **Letters & Faxes** tab. *See Figure 28.*

➤ *3.* Click once on the desired template name. For example, click once on **Professional Fax**.

➤ *4.* In the Create New area, select the **Template** option.

➤ *5.* Select **OK**.

➤ *6.* Edit the template elements as desired.

➤ *7.* When all the changes have been made to the template elements, select the **Save** button. The Templates folder should be displayed. Type the template name. Select **Save**.

Note: The new template name displays in the title bar.

Figure 28.
New dialog box with Letters & Faxes tab forward.

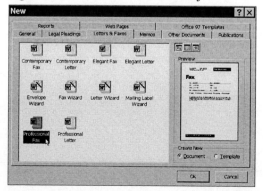

Set Tabs Using the Horizontal Ruler

➤ 1. In a document, place the insertion point at the location where tabs are to be set, or select the text for which tabs are to be set.

➤ 2. Check that the desired tab alignment symbol displays on the left side of the horizontal ruler. If necessary, click on the **Tab** button ⌊L⌋ until the desired tab alignment symbol displays. *See Figure 29.*

➤ 3. Move the mouse pointer to the desired position on the ruler and click to set the tab location.

➤ 4. To remove a tab, point to the tab on the ruler and click, hold, and drag the tab off the Ruler. Release the mouse button.

Note: *Tab settings apply only to the selected lines or to the line containing the insertion point.*

Figure 29
Horizontal ruler.

Tab button

Set Tabs Using the Tabs Dialog Box

➤ 1. Place the insertion point at the location where the tabs are to be set, or select the text for which tabs are to be set.
➤ 2. Select **Format**, **Tabs**. *See Figure 30.*
➤ 3. To set a tab, type the desired tab location in the Tab stop position: box.
➤ 4. To select a different tab alignment, move the mouse pointer to the Alignment area and click on the desired type.
➤ 5. Click the **Set** button.
➤ 6. Repeat for additional tabs. When finished, click **OK**. *To clear all tabs,* highlight the desired line(s), choose **Format**, **Tabs,** and choose the **Clear All** button.
➤ 7. Select **OK**.

Note: Tab settings apply only to the selected lines or to the line containing the insertion point.

Figure 30.
Tabs dialog box.

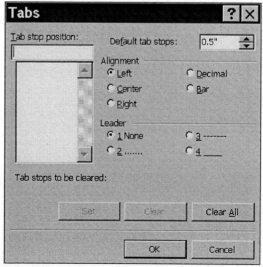

Control Text Flow
(Widow/Orphan Control, Keep Lines Together, or Keep With Next)

To keep lines together:

➤ *1.* Select all lines to be kept on one page. Go to step 3

To keep a line with the next line:

➤ *2.* Place the insertion point in the heading or sidehead that is located at the bottom of a page.

➤ *3.* Select **Format, Paragraph**.

➤ *4.* Click on the **Line and Page Breaks** tab. *See Figure 31.*

➤ *5.* In the Pagination section, select the desired option. (For example, select the **Keep with next** option to keep a side-head with the following paragraph.)

➤ *6.* Select **OK**.

Note: If nonprinting symbols are turned on, a small dark square displays in the left margin to indicate that special paragraph formatting has been applied to the text.

Figure 31. Paragraph dialog box with Line and Page Breaks tab forward.

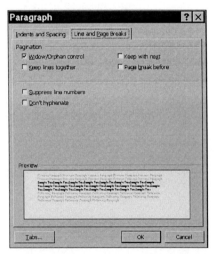

Create Bookmarks

➤ 1. Place the insertion point at the location where the bookmark will be inserted.
➤ 2. Select **Insert, Bookmark.**
➤ 3. Type the desired bookmark name.

Note: A bookmark name can be up to 40 characters (letters, numbers, and underscores), but no spaces.

➤ 4. Select **Add.**

*Note: No change displays in the document window. To view the bookmark indicator, select **Tools, Options.** On the View tab, select the **Bookmarks** option in the Show area. Select **OK.** A large I-beam displays at the location where the bookmark was created.*

Go to a Bookmark

➤ 1. Select **Edit, Go To.**

Note: The Find and Replace dialog box displays with the Go To tab selected.

➤ 2. In the Go to what: box, select **Bookmark.**
➤ 3. Click on the down arrow beside the Enter bookmark name: box and select the desired bookmark name.
➤ 4. Select **Go To.**

Note: The insertion point moves to the selected bookmark in the document. The Go To dialog box remains on the screen to allow you to select another bookmark location if desired.

➤ 5. Select **Close** to exit the Find and Replace dialog box.

Create a Watermark

➤ *1.* Select **View, Header and Footer**.

Note: The Header and Footer toolbar displays, and the Header and Footer areas display at the top and bottom of the document window. (If necessary, move the Header and Footer Toolbar above the Header area.) A header is used for a watermark so the Watermark will print on more than one page (if desired).

➤ *2.* Select Inset, Picture and choose the desired picture/graphic image.

Note: The graphic image displays in the Header area.

➤ *3.* Move the mouse pointer onto the graphic image and click once to select the image.

*Note: The Picture toolbar displays. If the Picture toolbar is not displayed, move the mouse pointer onto the graphic image, click the right mouse button, and select **Show Picture Toolbar**.*

➤ *4.* Select the **Format Picture** button 🖼 on the Picture toolbar. *See Figure 32.*

➤ *5.* Select the **Layout** tab. In the Wrapping style area, click on **Behind** text; click **OK**.

➤ *6.* On the Picture toolbar, select the **Image Control** button ▣ and choose the **Watermark** option. *See Figure 33.*

Note: The image changes to a light-gray color.

➤ *7.* Select the graphic. Small boxes display at the corners and edges of the border. (If necessary, click on the graphic image.) With the four-headed arrow displayed, drag the watermark to the desired location on the page.

➤ *8.* Close the Header and Footer toolbar.

Note: *The Picture toolbar is also removed from the screen when you close the Header and Footer toolbar.*

➤ *9.* Type and format text. The text will display on top of the watermark.

Figure 32.
Format Picture button on the Picture toolbar.

Figure 33.
Image Control options on the Picture toolbar.

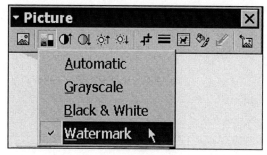

Use Hidden Text

Note: The Show/Hide button should be on. If necessary, select the Show/Hide Button on the Standard toolbar.

➤ *1.* Highlight the text to be hidden.

➤ *2.* Click on **Format, Font.**

➤ *3.* On the Font tab, choose **Hidden in the Effects** area.

Note: A dotted underline displays below the text formatted as hidden.

➤ *4.* Select the **Show/Hide** button to turn off the nonprinting characters.

Note: The hidden text will not display when the nonprinting characters are turned off. Also, the hidden text will not print.

To unhide the text:

➤ Turn the nonprinting characters on, i.e., select the **Show/Hide** button on the Standard toolbar.

Figure 34.
Clipboard toolbar.

Collect and Paste Items to the Clipboard

Note: The document with the text or objects to be copied should be open and displayed on the screen.

➤ 1. View the Clipboard toolbar. Right-click on any toolbar and choose Clipboard. *See Figure 34 on page 54..*

➤ 2. Highlight the text or select the object to be copied.

➤ 3. Click on the Copy button in the Clipboard toolbar or in the Standard toolbar.

➤ 4. Repeat steps 2 and 3 and continue to highlight and copy the desired text or object.

Note: An icon displays in the Clipboard toolbar for each copied item. The clipboard toolbar can hold up to twelve copied items.

➤ 5. To relocate the copied text or objects, place the insertion point in the desired location in the open document, new document, or other Office program where the copied text or objects are to be located.

➤ 6. Click on the icon containing the desired text or objects in the Clipboard toolbar. Or click on the Paste All button to retrieve all the copied text or objects.

Note: To clear the Clipboard, click on the Clear Clipboard button. Close the Clipboard toolbar, when desired.

Notes:

Microsoft Word 2000 In Layman's Terms

Glossary for Microsoft Word® 2000

In Layman's Terms

Active document – The document that is currently in the window.

Active window – The window that is currently in use.

Alignment – The horizontal and vertical position of text in relation to the page, or in relation to a table cell.

Arrow keys – The keys used to move the insertion point or select from a menu or list.

Ascending – Sorting a list from A-Z or a numbered list from 1-10, etc.

Body text – One of more lines of text that generally wrap around in a paragraph format. Examples of body text are the paragraphs containing the message of a letter of memorandum.

Bookmark – A bookmark is used to electronically mark a specific location in a document similar to placing a bookmark in a book.

Boot up – The PC start up of a computer.

Border – The printed rules placed around text or the page.

Bullet – A symbol placed at the beginning of each line in a list to distinguish each item.

Button – A small square area that can be clicked on to perform an action. For example, a Toolbar contains various buttons.

Cascade – Windows that overlap showing the title bars. The active window is on top.

Cell – The basic unit of a table formed when a row and a column intersect.

Character spacing – Used to increase or decrease the amount of space between letters in selected text. Also referred to as tracking.

Click – To press the left or primary mouse button once.

Clipboard – A temporary storage place for information, that has been cut or copied.

Close – To end the program or window in which you are working.

Column – A vertical section of a table or worksheet.

Command – The instruction that causes action on the part of the program.

Comments – Comments are electronic notes placed in a document, similar to writing a note on a "Post-it" form.

Copy – To duplicate information or graphics that are to be placed in another location.

Crop – To cut away parts of a graphic or picture.

Cut – To remove information from a document and relocate the information elsewhere.

Data – A set of information.

Data source file (database) – A file that contains the information for a merge document.

Default – A predefined setting that the program returns to each time you open a new document.

Delete – To remove information or a file.

Descending – To sort a list in reverse order, such as Z-A or 10-1.

Desktop – The screen that represents your work area. This is the area that displays icons, the task bar, and windows.

Dialog box – The box that appears when you need to make additional choices after you choose a command.

Disk – A round flat piece of flexible plastic or inflexible metal that stores data.

Disk drive – The part of the computer where the disk can be accessed.

Document – The file that can be worked on, saved, or accessed from a program.

Document window – The window that contains the document.

Double-click – Press the left or primary mouse button twice rapidly.

Drag & Drop – The process of moving or copying information from one location to another using the mouse.

Edit – To add, delete, or change information that has already been entered.

Electronic mail (e-mail) – The use of telecommunications or network services to send notes, messages, or files to a different computer.

Filename – A title given to a file used to identify the file for future retrieval

Folder – An electronic location where files are stored.

Font – The style of type used for typing and printing.

Footer – The information placed at the bottom of each page to identify the page; it is often the same on every page.

Footnote – A reference placed at the bottom of the page or at the end of a document that has been referred to in the document.

Format – To prepare a disk to receive information. Also, the way text appears on a page, such as bold, typeface, indention, etc.

Gridlines – The lines that define cells in a table when there are no borders selected.

Handles – The small boxes used to resize an object when that object is selected.

Header – The information placed at the top of each document page.

Help – The place where you can get instructions on how to perform a certain task.

Highlighting – The process of selecting text on the screen. The text usually displays with a dark background.

HTML (Hypertext Markup Language) – The set of rules and codes that is used on the World Wide Web (Internet).

Icon – A small graphic used to represent an object or program that when clicked on will open the program or object.

Insertion point – The blinking vertical line located where the text or graphic will be inserted.

Install – To prepare a program or equipment for first-time use; transferring a program from the CD or disk(s) to the computer's hard drive.

Internet – The World Wide Web (WWW), connecting millions of computers together to share information.

Intranet – The inner business connection of computers. May or may not be connected to the Internet.

Kerning – Adjusting the horizontal space between a pair of characters.

Landscape – The layout of a page having the long edge at the top and bottom and the short edges on the sides.

List – The options that drop down on the screen after clicking on a menu name or fill-in area in a dialog box.

Main document – A document used to merge with a data source. The main document contains merge fields to represent the text that will vary in each merged document.

Margin – The boundaries of text or graphics on a page.

Maximize – The act of making a window expand to the maximum the program and screen allow.

Menu – A list of available options.

Merge – To combine variable information with information that remains unchanged.

Merge field – The placeholder in a main document that is replaced by information from the data source.

Minimize – To contract a window to an icon, leaving that window open but not active.

Modem – The device used to connect a computer to a phone line. A modem translates analog signals to digital signals and visa versa.

Monitor – A television-like device used to view signals from the computer.

Mouse Pointer – The symbol on the screen that displays when the mouse device is moved.

Move – To transfer information from one place to another.

Nonprinting symbols – Symbols that display on the screen but do not print. The nonprinting symbols are turned on or off by clicking on the Show/Hide button.

Office Assistant – An animated icon used to access the Help feature of a program.

Online – Being connected to the World Wide Web (Internet) through your ISP (Internet Service Provider).

Page break – The command placed on a page to require that the following text be placed on the next page.

Password – The word or phrase used to gain entry into a protected document or program.

Paste – Insert cut or copied text or graphics into a document.

Point – The unit of measurement of character height. There are 72 points to an inch.

Portrait – The layout of a page with the short edge at the top and bottom and the long edge on each side.

Program – Computer software that contains instructions to tell the computer what to do.

Prompt – An indication that the computer needs more information to proceed.

Query – A request for a certain type of data.

Read-only document – A document that can be opened and modified but must be saved with a new filename. This feature is used to protect a document from being changed and saved over the original file.

Recycle Bin – A temporary holding place for deleted files. To permanently delete the files, the recycle bin must be emptied.

Right-mouse click – The act of pressing the secondary mouse button (usually located on the right side of the mouse).

Row – A horizontal section of a worksheet.

Ruler – A bar used for measurement that is displayed in a document window.

Save – To place documents into a file for future use.

Scroll – To move horizontally or vertically in a window.

Select – The process of highlighting text.

Shortcut menu – A menu list that appears when you right mouse click while pointing at certain areas.

Side-head – A title for paragraph(s) that is typed on a separate line.

Subscript – A character printed slightly below adjacent characters, e.g., H_2O.

Superscript – A character printed slightly above adjacent characters, e.g. 32°.

Template – A template is a model for a document. A template stores information on how to format a document, such as margins and borders.

Toolbar – A collection of buttons. The buttons are shortcuts to activate many menu options.

Track changes – The track changes feature is used to automatically mark changes made to text. For example, two different users can insert and/or delete text in the same document. The deleted text is marked by a line drawn through it (the strike through font effect). Added text is shown in a color.

Tracking – See Character spacing.

Virus – A program that attaches itself to another program waiting for the right command to activate. It then can spread throughout your computer destroying programs and files.

Watermark – Text or a graphic image that is printed in a light gray or light color. Other text and/or a graphic image can be placed on top of the watermark image.

Web address – The path to a Web site on the Internet.

Web browser – The program used to view the Internet pages (Web sites).

Web page – A document placed on the Internet as part of a Web site.

Web site – A specific place on the World Wide Web representing a person or business.

Wizard – A tool that asks you questions so it can assist you in performing a task, such as formatting a letterhead.

Word wrap – The function that automatically continues text on the next line when the insertion point reaches the right margin.

WordArt – A special technique used to make effects with text. For example, text can be printed in a curved format rather than printed in a straight line.

World Wide Web – The collection of web sites available through computer connections all over the world.

Index

AutoCorrect, 36
AutoFormat, 37
AutoText, 39

Bookmark
    Create, 51
    Cross-reference, 35
    Go to a Bookmark, 51
Bullet or Number a List, 11

Click & Type, 46
Collect and Paste Items
    to the Clipboard, 55
Columns, *see also tables*
    Create Newspaper-Style, 21
Comments, 43
Copy Text using Drag & Drop, 3
Create a Watermark, 52

Document Versions, 6

Favorites Folder, 28
Files
    Copy, 26
    Delete, 27
    Find, 27
    Move, 26
    Rename, 26
Flier Using AutoShapes, 38
Folder, Create New, 27
Font Size and/or Appearance, 46
Footers, 29
Form Letter
    Database, 30
    Labels from a Database, 34

Main Document, 32
Merge Main Document
    with Data Source files, 33
Format Painter, 22

Grammar Feature, 24
Graphic Image, Insert, 46

Headers, 28
Help Wizard Assistant, 8
Hidden Text, 54

Letterhead with Borders, 37

Macros, 40
Margins, 9, 45
Memo Wizard, 10
Move Text Using Drag & Drop, 3
Move to Beginning Document, 3
Move to End of Document, 3

New Folder, 27
Number or Bullet a List, 11
Number Pages Automatically, 25

Open an Existing Document, 4

Password
    Open a Password-
        Protected File, 5
    Remove a Password, 6
    Save with a Password, 4
Picture, Insert, 46

Print
    Envelope address, 13
    Comments, 43
Read-Only Documents, 44
Redo Command, 11
Rename Files, Using the Open
    or Save Dialog box, 26

Save and Save As, 7
Select (Highlight)
    Extend a Selection, 2
    One Line, 1
    Paragraph, 1
    Sentence, 1
    All Text, 1
    A Word, 1
Send To, 27
Shrink to Fit, 22
Spelling Feature, 23
Subscript, 40
Superscript, 40

Table Borders, remove, 17
Tables
    Calculate a Column
      or Row, 20
    Center Horizontally &
      Vertically, 19
    Change Column Widths, 18
    Create, 14
    Delete a Column, 16
    Delete a Row, 15
    Insert a Column, 15
    Insert a Row, 15
    Merge Cells, 17
    Move a Column, 16
    Remove Borders, 17
    Set Row Height, 18
    Sort Rows, 19
    Use Underlines, 21
Tabs
    Set Using the Horizontal
      Ruler, 48
    Set Using the Tabs Dialog
      Box, 49

Templates, 47
Text
    Delete, 2
    Hidden, 54
    Indent, 12
    Insert, 3
    Replace, 10
    Select, 1
Text Flow
    Control of, 50
    Widow/Orphan control and
      Keep lines together, 50
Thesaurus, 24
Toolbars
    Customize, 44
    Display a Different, 17
Track Changes, 42

Undo Command, 11

Vertical Line Spacing
    Change, 25

Watermark
    Create, 52
Window
    Close, All Windows, 4
    Open, 4
Wizards
    Help Wizard Assistant, 8
    Memo Wizard, 10
Word Count, 22
WordArt, 14

Microsoft Word® 2000 Toolbars

Standard Toolbar

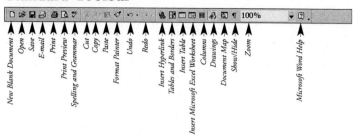

New Blank Document, Open, Save, E-mail, Print, Print Preview, Spelling and Grammar, Cut, Copy, Paste, Format Painter, Undo, Redo, Insert Hyperlink, Tables and Borders, Insert Table, Insert Microsoft Excel Worksheet, Columns, Drawings, Document Map, Show/Hide, Zoom, Microsoft Word Help

Formatting Toolbar

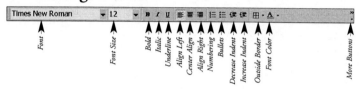

Font, Font Size, Bold, Italic, Underline, Align Left, Center Align, Align Right, Numbering, Bullets, Decrease Indent, Increase Indent, Outside Border, Font Color, More Buttons

Status Bar

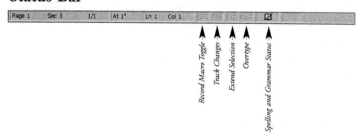

Record Macro Toggle, Track Changes, Extend Selection, Overtype, Spelling and Grammar Status

Drawing Toolbar

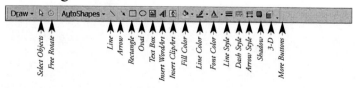

Select Objects, Free Rotate, Line, Arrow, Rectangle, Oval, Text Box, Insert WordArt, Insert ClipArt, Fill Color, Line Color, Font Color, Line Style, Dash Style, Arrow Style, Shadow, 3-D, More Buttons

Great Values!

In Layman's Terms

Microsoft Office 2000 Essentials In Layman's Terms Includes: Word, Excel, Access, & PowerPoint	$39.99
Microsoft Office 2000 Pro In Layman's Terms Includes: Word, Excel, Access, PowerPoint, & Windows	$49.99
Microsoft Word 2000 In Layman's Terms	$12.99
Microsoft Excel 2000 In Layman's Terms	$12.99
Microsoft Access 2000 In Layman's Terms	$12.99
Microsoft PowerPoint 2000 In Layman's Terms	$12.99
Microsoft Windows 2000 In Layman's Terms	$12.99
Internet and Email Tips In Layman's Terms	$9.99

(All prices in U.S. Funds. In California add sales tax of 7.25%.)

Fax or Mail Order Form

Computers Made Easy
PO Box 98
Hollister, CA 95024-0098

Fax: 831-636-6813 (Fax this form.)
Local Voice: 831-636-6938
Telephone Orders: 800-484-9998 x5511
Have Credit Card Ready
Email Orders: LaymansTerms@usa.net

Name   Company Name:

Street Address for shipping:

City: State: Zip:

Area Code: Phone number: Fax No:

Email Address:

Visa/Master Card No.:   Expiration Date:

Complete Name on Credit Card:

Signature:

Name of Book	Quantity	Price	Sub-Total

Shipping Charges:
US: $3.00 for first book & $2.00 for each additional book;
$5.00 for MS Office Essentials or Pro
International: $8.00 for first book & $4.00 for each additional book;
$9.00 for MS Office Essentials or Pro (Estimate) US Funds

California Sales Tax 7.25%	
Shipping Charges	
Total	

Great Values!

In Layman's Terms

Microsoft Office 2000 Essentials In Layman's Terms	
Includes: Word, Excel, Access, & PowerPoint	$39.99
Microsoft Office 2000 Pro In Layman's Terms	
Includes: Word, Excel, Access, PowerPoint, & Windows	$49.99
Microsoft Word 2000 In Layman's Terms	$12.99
Microsoft Excel 2000 In Layman's Terms	$12.99
Microsoft Access 2000 In Layman's Terms	$12.99
Microsoft PowerPoint 2000 In Layman's Terms	$12.99
Microsoft Windows 2000 In Layman's Terms	$12.99
Internet and Email Tips In Layman's Terms	$9.99

(All prices in U.S. Funds. In California add sales tax of 7.25%.)

Fax or Mail Order Form
Computers Made Easy
PO Box 98
Hollister, CA 95024-0098

Fax: 831-636-6813 (Fax this form.)
Local Voice: 831-636-6938
Telephone Orders: 800-484-9998 x5511
Have Credit Card Ready
Email Orders: LaymansTerms@usa.net

Name   Company Name:

Street Address for shipping:

City: State: Zip:

Area Code: Phone number: Fax No:

Email Address:

Visa/Master Card No.:   Expiration Date:

Complete Name on Credit Card:

Signature:

Name of Book	Quantity	Price	Sub-Total

Shipping Charges:
US: $3.00 for first book & $2.00 for each additional book;
$5.00 for MS Office Essentials or Pro
International: $8.00 for first book & $4.00 for each additional book;
$9.00 for MS Office Essentials or Pro (Estimate) US Funds

California Sales Tax 7.25%	
Shipping Charges	
Total	

Great Values!

In Layman's Terms

Microsoft Office 2000 Essentials In Layman's Terms	$39.99
Includes: Word, Excel, Access, & PowerPoint	
Microsoft Office 2000 Pro In Layman's Terms	$49.99
Includes: Word, Excel, Access, PowerPoint, & Windows	
Microsoft Word 2000 In Layman's Terms	$12.99
Microsoft Excel 2000 In Layman's Terms	$12.99
Microsoft Access 2000 In Layman's Terms	$12.99
Microsoft PowerPoint 2000 In Layman's Terms	$12.99
Microsoft Windows 2000 In Layman's Terms	$12.99
Internet and Email Tips In Layman's Terms	$9.99

(All prices in U.S. Funds. In California add sales tax of 7.25%.)

Fax or Mail Order Form

Computers Made Easy
PO Box 98
Hollister, CA 95024-0098

Fax: 831-636-6813 (Fax this form.)
Local Voice: 831-636-6938
Telephone Orders: 800-484-9998 x5511
Have Credit Card Ready
Email Orders: LaymansTerms@usa.net

Name   Company Name:

Street Address for shipping:

City: State: Zip:

Area Code: Phone number: Fax No:

Email Address:

Visa/Master Card No.:   Expiration Date:

Complete Name on Credit Card:

Signature:

Name of Book	Quantity	Price	Sub-Total

Shipping Charges:
US: $3.00 for first book & $2.00 for each additional book;
$5.00 for MS Office Essentials or Pro
International: $8.00 for first book & $4.00 for each additional book;
$9.00 for MS Office Essentials or Pro (Estimate) US Funds

California Sales Tax 7.25%	
Shipping Charges	
Total